This book belongs to

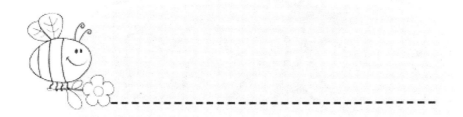

English - Greek

duck Date _____

πάπια

duck   πάπια

duck
duck
duck
duck
duck

Make a sentence

horse   Date _____

άλογο

horse · άλογο

horse
horse
horse
horse
horse

Make a sentence

mouse   Date _____

ποντίκια

mouse — ποντίκια

mouse
mouse
mouse
mouse
mouse

Make a sentence

wolf   Date _____

λύκος

wolf   λύκος

wolf

wolf

wolf

wolf

wolf

Make a sentence

panda   Date _____

γιγάντιο πάντα ☆☆☆

panda   γιγάντιο πάντα

Make a sentence

chicken   Date _____

κοτόπουλο

chicken κοτόπουλο

chicken
chicken
chicken
chicken
chicken

Make a sentence

dinosaur Date _____

δεινόσαυρος

dinosaur   δεινόσαυρος

dinosaur

dinosaur

dinosaur

dinosaur

dinosaur

Make a sentence

elephant Date _____

ελέφαντας

elephant ελέφαντας

elephant
elephant
elephant
elephant
elephant

Make a sentence

cow   Date _____

αγελάδα   

cow   αγελάδα

cow
cow
cow
cow
cow

Make a sentence

butterfly   Date _____

πεταλούδα

butterfly πεταλούδα

butterfly
butterfly
butterfly
butterfly
butterfly

Make a sentence

worm   Date _____

σκουλήκι

worm   σκουλήκι

worm

worm

worm

worm

worm

Make a sentence

puppy   Date _____

κουτάβι

puppy κουτάβι

puppy
puppy
puppy
puppy
puppy

Make a sentence

turtle Date _____

χελώνα

turtle   χελώνα

turtle
turtle
turtle
turtle
turtle

Make a sentence

turkey Date _____

Τουρκία

turkey Τουρκία

turkey
turkey
turkey
turkey
turkey

Make a sentence

hippopotamus　　　Date _____

ιπποπόταμος

hippopotamus ιπποπόταμος

hippopotamus

hippopotamus

hippopotamus

hippopotamus

hippopotamus

Make a sentence

tiger Date _____

τίγρη

tiger   τίγρη

tiger
tiger
tiger
tiger
tiger

Make a sentence

hen   Date _____

κότα

hen κότα

Make a sentence

alligator   Date _____

αλλιγάτορας

alligator   αλλιγάτορας

alligator   ....
alligator   ....
alligator   ....
alligator   ....
alligator   ....

Make a sentence

monkey   Date _____

Πίθηκος   

monkey   Πίθηκος

Make a sentence

spider Date _____

αράχνη

spider　　　αράχνη

spider
spider
spider
spider
spider

Make a sentence

shark Date_____

καρχαρίας

shark   καρχαρίας

shark
shark
shark
shark
shark

Make a sentence

lion   Date _____

λιοντάρι

lion

λιοντάρι

Make a sentence

snail Date _____

σαλιγκάρι

snail σαλιγκάρι

snail
snail
snail
snail
snail

Make a sentence

kangaroo Date _____

καγκουρώ

kangaroo καγκουρώ

kangaroo
kangaroo
kangaroo
kangaroo
kangaroo

Make a sentence

fox   Date _____

αλεπού   

fox — αλεπού

Make a sentence

snake Date _____

φίδι

snake   φίδι

snake
snake
snake
snake
snake

Make a sentence

camel Date _____

καμήλα

camel   καμήλα

camel
camel
camel
camel
camel

Make a sentence

octopus   Date_____

χταπόδι

octopus χταπόδι

octopus
octopus
octopus
octopus
octopus

Make a sentence

rooster Date_____

πετεινός

rooster

πετεινός

rooster

rooster

rooster

rooster

rooster

Make a sentence

kitten   Date_____

γατάκι

kitten γατάκι

kitten
kitten
kitten
kitten
kitten

Make a sentence

deer   Date _____

ελάφι

deer   ελάφι

Make a sentence

ant Date_____

μυρμήγκι

ant　　　　　　　　　μυρμήγκι

ant
ant
ant
ant
ant

Make a sentence

dog Date _____

σκύλος

dog   σκύλος

dog
dog
dog
dog
dog

Make a sentence

giraffe   Date_____

καμηλοπάρδαλη

giraffe   καμηλοπάρδαλη

giraffe
giraffe
giraffe
giraffe
giraffe

Make a sentence

cat   Date_____

Γάτα

cat Γάτα

cat
cat
cat
cat
cat

Make a sentence

crab Date _____

Κάβουρας

crab   Κάβουρας

crab

crab

crab

crab

crab

Make a sentence

zebra   Date _____

ζέβρα

zebra   ζέβρα

zebra
zebra
zebra
zebra
zebra

Make a sentence

eagle   Date _____

αετός   ☆☆☆

eagle αετός

eagle eagle
eagle eagle
eagle eagle
eagle eagle
eagle eagle

Make a sentence

rabbit Date_____

κουνέλι

rabbit   κουνέλι

rabbit

rabbit

rabbit

rabbit

rabbit

Make a sentence

sheep Date _____

πρόβατο

sheep πρόβατο

Make a sentence

fish   Date_____

ψάρι   

fish ψάρι

fish
fish
fish
fish
fish

Make a sentence

bird   Date _____

πουλί   

bird

bird
bird
bird
bird
bird

πουλί

Make a sentence

dolphin Date_____

δελφίνι

dolphin δελφίνι

dolphin

dolphin

dolphin

dolphin

dolphin

Make a sentence

bee   Date _____

μέλισσα

bee μέλισσα

Make a sentence

hedgehog Date_____

Σκατζόχοιρος

hedgehog   Σκατζόχοιρος

hedgehog

hedgehog

hedgehog

hedgehog

hedgehog

Make a sentence

lobster   Date_____

αστακός   

lobster   αστακός

lobster

lobster

lobster

lobster

lobster

Make a sentence

owl   Date _____

κουκουβάγια

owl

owl
owl
owl
owl
owl

κουκουβάγια

Make a sentence

frog   Date_____

βάτραχος

frog   βάτραχος

Make a sentence

pig Date _____

Χοίρος

pig

Χοίρος

Make a sentence

goat Date _____

γίδα

goat   γίδα

goat
goat
goat
goat
goat

Make a sentence

dragonfly Date _____

λιβελούλα

dragonfly   λιβελούλα

dragonfly

dragonfly

dragonfly

dragonfly

dragonfly

Make a sentence

squirrel Date_____

σκίουρος

squirrel　　　　σκίουρος

Make a sentence

parrot   Date _____

παπαγάλος   

parrot παπαγάλος

parrot
parrot
parrot
parrot
parrot

Make a sentence

Made in the USA
Middletown, DE
14 March 2021